The Educator's 180-Day Gratitude Turnaround

The Educator's 180-Day Gratitude Turnaround
Self-Reflection Journal

Jenny Severson, EdD

Endorsements for Dr. Jenny Severson and *The Educator's 180-Day Gratitude Turnaround*

"There is not a single person I know, not one, that thrives in a culture of negativity. Positive school, office, and home cultures are built on the bedrock of optimistic attitudes, clear heads, and grateful hearts. Dr. Severson offers a tangible resource for reconnecting with gratitude via daily reflections on life and joyful quotes culled from people we've come to know and love. Let this book be your daily dose of pause, reflect, and reconnect time in the midst of an otherwise chaotic time."
Weston Kieschnick
Associate Partner, International Center
for Leadership in Education

"What if we possessed a power that would enrich our lives, enhance our relationships and experiences, and even strengthen our physical, emotional, and mental health, but didn't know we had that power? In this simple yet profound book, Jenny reminds us each day of the power of gratitude and how we can use it to thrive and flourish throughout our life's journey."
Paul Bernabei
Author, Director, Top 20 Training

"Incorporating an attitude of gratitude changes us, those around us, and our futures. What Jenny has done here is provide us with a tool that helps us to build habits of the heart. By emphasizing these repeated practices, we're actually giving ourselves gifts—the gift of optimism, the gift of grace, the gift of love."
Pete Hall
President, Strive Success Solutions

"The educational system is a grind. Many of us embrace that grind because we are attracted to work that is difficult, that requires spiritual grit, that interfaces us with human fragility and beauty in its most raw moments. We need coaches and anchors and friends who believe in us. Jenny Severson believes in us. Collectively with her mentors, she nudges, consoles, speaks truth, and whispers simple clear wisdom in small digestible morsels. Keep this book on your desk. Gift it to a friend and your child's teachers. Share quotes with your team, class, family. Together we can be grateful for such important work in this world."
Patti Brucki
Librarian, Thornwood High School, South Holland, Ilinois

"Jenny's sincerity in sharing her personal story and insights is both inspirational and motivating. In challenging times, it's especially helpful to have a nudge toward self-care and the importance of bringing joy and gratitude into our lives."
Bobbi DePorter
President, Quantum Learning Network; Author

"I began the gratitude pathway in 2006; it has been one of the top 10 difference-making paths for me. This might be a powerful journey for you if you feel your path is unclear, with slippery steps just a bit too far apart. Jump in and enjoy the growing."
Dr. Eric Jensen
Jensen Learning, Author

Copyright © 2020 by Jenny Severson, EdD
All rights reserved. This book contains material protected under international and federal copyright laws and treaties. Any unauthorized reprint or use of this material is prohibited. No parts of this book may be reproduced or transmitted in any form or by any means, electronic or mechanical, including photocopying, recording, or by any other information storage and retrieval system without express written consent by the author/publisher.

ISBN: 979-8-665-32235-3

Cover design: Carrie Carlson

This book was published by Ripple Press.

Printed in the United States of America

*For Todd, Lucy, Zoey, and Henry,
and educators around the world.
I'm forever grateful for your tenacity and calm spirit.*

Contents

Meet Dr. Jenny Severson, EdD   xi
Preface   xiii
Introduction   xv
My Story   xvii
My ABC's of Gratitude   xxix
Self-Reflection Journal   1
Closing Thoughts   181
Pass It On   183

Meet Dr. Jenny Severson, EdD
Educator, Author, Speaker

Dr. Jenny Severson is an educational consultant who embraces a love of learning and teaching. She's been a classroom teacher, school principal, and worked with hundreds of schools in staff development.

Jetting across the globe with Quantum Learning Education, she's reached almost every state and more than a dozen countries. Her recent book, *Thrive*, co-authored with her speaker sisters, takes you on the hero's journey as an educator.

Jenny played college basketball at Lake Forest (Illinois) College and was part of two state championship runs at Madison East High School in Madison, Wisconsin. She's a mom of three children; married to the love of her life, Todd Johnson; and a breast cancer survivor.

Join us on the road to gratitude as we dive into 180 days of overlooked blessing and thankful hearts.

To connect with Jenny to speak at your school or organization, contact her at:
 Web site: JennySeverson.com
 Email: Jeniferjseverson@gmail.com
 Facebook: Jenny Severson
 Instagram: @dr.jenny.severson
 Twitter: @severson_j

Preface

Who doesn't need a buffer against today's headwinds? Educators are uniquely gifted with student interactions and a community of learners. We can intentionally pour into and develop this community to receive connections, affirmation, and growth. As teachers, all of that is at our fingertips, depending on our focus and intent.

Think of this book—and your journal—as a practical tool for both you and your students. You write into it, and you and, potentially, your students reap the benefits. This is your time; this is your tool. Start where you are. Start today. Gratitude will change your life forever.

Gratitude and Optimism are antidotes to chronic stress and toxic positivity, and they come with some very basic rules:

The Problem: Rules of Chronic Stress:
1. Stress starts with effects on your motivation.
2. Being in close contact with stressed people causes increased stress levels for you.
3. Stress impairs self-control.
4. Stress impairs memory.
5. The hippocampus is smaller in people with chronic stress.
6. Dwelling on stress causes inflammation in the body where the amygdala modulates the fear response highly activated in times of stress.

The Solution: Align Gratitude with These Factors:
1. Self-awareness
2. Strong habits in stress prevention

3. Toxic stress resistance (With whom are you hanging around?)
4. Reliable resilience (community, connection, and belonging)
5. Alignment of stress beliefs and actions creates sizzling new connections in your brain.
6. Optimism factor—keeps you healthier, period! Optimism is not delusional; it's believing life is better on the other side. It's shifting perspective. Our reality is personal; we create it every day.

How we show up matters. So, let's suit up and show up with this powerful tool of gratitude as you start your new school year.

Introduction

Let me share a powerful parable about how gratitude can change the course of your destiny in a heartbeat.

Times were tough, and two men were walking side by side. Both were poor farmers grumbling about how tough life was. Along the way they met their rabbi, who asked, "How is it for you?"

The first man said, "Lousy, awful," bemoaning his lot and lack. What none of them knew was that God was eavesdropping on their conversation, at this point thinking, *You think your life is lousy now. I'll show you what lousy is!*

Then the rabbi turned to the other man and said, "How is it for you, my friend?"

"Ah, Rabbi, life is so good. God is so gracious, so generous. Each morning when I awaken, I'm so grateful for the gift of another day for I know, rain or shine, it will unfold in wonder and blessing too bountiful to count. Life is so very good."

Hearing this, God smiled as the second man's thanksgiving soared upward until it became one with the harmony of the heavenly hosts. The Almighty roared with loud laughter, "Good? You think your life is good now? I'll show you what good is!"

Gratitude is one of the most passionate transformative forces in the universe. When we offer thanks to God or to another person, gratitude rewards us with renewal. And, connection. We are hardwired to connect.

Gratitude held me together when everything was falling apart. And it works in life's small and large moments, providing us with a powerful antidote to the landscape of our lives.

The Bible instructs us to "give thanks in all circumstances," but it doesn't tell us we have to be smiling when we say it! In fact, many times over the years I have found that sitting still more often, living in the pause of life to renew myself, is just the space needed to keep charging ahead. One day at a time. One small step each day. In thanks!

My Story

Gratitude is found in sparks of joy and in the depths of despair.

We all have a moment in time that defines us—a story.

While there are many accomplishments I (and my ego) would love to share, it was truly the worst year of my life that taught me the most and is the reason for this book. That year taught me courage, how to pivot, and how to own my life in new ways I'd never experienced before. My worst year is now a story for which I am truly grateful, every day. We typically don't act when in our comfort zone; we act when we are pushed out into new domains. Here's one way how that looked for me over a ten-month period:

The timeline:

- I found a small lump on the left side of my breast while stretching in October 2017.
- I woke up the next day and knew something wasn't right.
- I had the lump biopsied in November 2017.
- I found out December 26, 2017, that I had breast cancer.
- On January 2, 2018, we met with the doctors.
- On January 12, I had surgery to remove the mass (the surgery was a success; we caught it early and nothing had spread).
- The mass was sent for testing, and we waited for the results.
- On February 1, my dad died. He was 74 years old.
- On February 7, we held my dad's funeral.
- On February 21 (which would have been my dad's 75th birthday), I found out from my doctors that I needed both chemotherapy and radiation because the removed mass and

the cells were very chaotic. . . . I had an Oncatype score of 28 (under 18 avoids chemo, in my case).
- On February 26, I started chemotherapy.
- On March 14, all my hair fell out.
- I was bald, sick, and nearly dead (at least that's how I felt) for the next three months.
- In March, April, and May, I continued going through more chemo, illness, and life navigation.
- I finished radiation on Monday, July 28, and moved back from Cleveland to Minnesota on September 7, 2018.

The timeline neglects to mention the "loneliness" factor. We had neither quality time to formulate a close circle of friends nor family physically around us during this time because we had just moved to a new state (fourteen hours away) several months earlier. We had moved for my husband's career which was a blessing. However, the loneliness of separating from deep friendships and relationships of the last decade was so hard. Everyone we knew (including us) put on a happy face and said, "You'll be great," "You guys are so social," "You'll find friends right away and a church home." Inside we were all grieving and in denial. We couldn't see it at the time, but this illness was going to grow us in a way we'd never imagined.

Life felt desperate, dark, and full of uncertainty. Lonely, afraid, and with no sense of belonging, I shut down. I was in self-protection mode. This is why now, today, my community of close friends is so very crucial to my health and wellness. Whomever I interact with, I ask myself, *How can I add value to them? Are we filling each other's buckets? Are they a person whose energy I can navigate? Are they grateful? What's the intention of this interaction? What's the motive behind the conversation, event, and/or connection?* Intention is everything to me now. I pray to never go back to a casual, haphazard style of interacting. It's not worth it.

My Story

After March 2018, I knew I had *very* good chances of coming out okay, which was hugely helpful. In fact, by taking the actions we did, there is a very low, single-digit chance of recurrence compared to the 40 percent chance normally expected for someone in my situation. Numbers can create relief. However, there was a long time (December 26, 2017, to March 26, 2018, to be exact) when I wasn't clear on what my outcomes would be. *This* was my personal pandemic. The feelings and situation of 2020 with the coronavirus brought to the surface *so many* of the same feelings, thoughts, and uncertainties I had gone through two years earlier. I share that because the world, collectively and literally, can now, at this point in history like no other, relate to this. Uncertainty, fear, distress, change, new routines, interrupted patterns of life—these are all part of this experience.

So, if I were in your shoes, what would I do with this new kind of knowledge? Meaning, what can you do? Where do you begin? To answer that, I can tell you what I learned about change through my own experience. For things to change, I realized I must change. This means looking at how to take care of myself so that I could live the life God intended. My faith was showing me the path toward new hope. As I explored and reflected on the difficult time I had experienced over the previous year, I realized that what lifted me out of this lonely, anxious, and dark experience were several things:

- God's grace; a second chance; faith
- Gratitude, optimism
- Curiosity

Let's focus on gratitude. What was there to be grateful for in this series of events?

There were actually dozens of things every day to be grateful for and attend to. More than ever I felt carried in a buoyant manner during this time, truly surrounded by God's love, direction, and presence. The more honest you are in your own life, the more willing and open you have to be when your life is cracked open—all the better for the climb back up. I call it, first, hitting rock bottom. Once you hit that rock, you can then rebuild. I hit the rock . . . that I know for sure. I was bald, sick, and nearly dead from these cancer treatments, my face flat on the floor as I prayed and asked for healing and gratitude. It was such a tricky time; for example, at my dad's funeral, there was no way I could tell anyone about my medical situation. I couldn't even process all the trauma of brokenness I was experiencing. Instead of talking to others, I talked to God. I wrote notes of thanks and gratitude to my creator. My rock.

I can now say with certainty that getting cancer, fighting cancer, and beating cancer have resulted in my living my life differently. As strange as it might seem, my struggle with cancer is one of the best things that has ever happened to me. Yes, I am grateful for breast cancer, because it has taught—and is still teaching—me so much about my life. The life I have ahead of me is a gift each and every day. When you stare at your own death, you realize the fragility of life. And you get busy creating new ways to thrive and live.

Before cancer, I was so "busy" with no margins, I mean like zero time in my life for self-care. I spent a lot of time people pleasing, performing, pretending, looking for approval from others, gaining titles and status, and running through airports nonstop. I was overweight in every way: physically, emotionally, spiritually. Being overwhelmed and overextended are recipes for chronic stress, and I experienced that toxicity firsthand. I stopped asking for what I needed. I failed to set boundaries and I was upset, irritable, and discontent.

Have you ever felt that way?

I now realize I have a daily choice to be in prevention. To be in company that is life-giving. To very carefully address boundaries, daily! I keep the gratitude rituals in place along with quiet prayer and meditation to be still and know there's something far greater than me working all things out for good. I'm

My Story

not casual about boundaries anymore. My life matters and so does yours. Brené Brown, researcher and storyteller, has a beautiful, simple way about boundaries, defining them as what's okay and what's not okay. I love that definition because I can use it with my kids, my husband, and people who ask me to do work projects, and it simplifies everything so beautifully.

Part of this journey for me is spiritual. A few people let me down during this time of my illness. They flat out ran in the other direction. They got scared. They didn't know how to reach out. I've forgiven all of it. I need you to know, though, frankly, there are people who run when things get tough. They are silent; there's fear instead of standing with you. Yet, here's another place where gratitude wins! It's amazing to reflect on the people who *did* show up for me and our family, and their acts of service and words of affirmation and love are sources of gratitude I will never forget.

Those who ran, it's okay, too. I get it. And I know too much about neuroscience to hold anyone at fault. That part of ruminating on old hurts is part of my past now. I let it go. You can, too. It takes some spiritual work. One great friend told me, "It's a spiritual axiom that whenever you are disturbed, the problem is with you, no one else, no other circumstance, nothing." Wow. That one really got me. It still does today. It's one of those statements in my memory bank that gets used sometimes every day. It's a way to pivot toward my values and toward what is good, pure, and right for me.

Another "drop-to-the-rock-bottom" moment happened in that statement for me. It's so fabulous to get to the heart right away in every instance that the "problem" is me . . . meaning I can change how I am responding to my life. For example, it could be time for a boundary check, community check, getting some bigger margin for rest, or exercise, or self-care. Checking in this way saves so much time, effort, and energy. For me, it's always one of these areas to improve or connect to and pivot. It's empowering because it leads me back to my choices!

The question is, How do we live in the pause? How can you and I stay centered on the action and mindset of gratitude, optimism, and hope? One centering action that guides us there is gratitude. When gratitude is not present, I can be optimistic. What is there to look forward to? Gratitude and optimism are like sister emotions. They walk hand in hand to connect us to love, peace, calm, and clarity of purpose—our True North.

Although gratitude and optimism go hand in hand, we sometimes separate them. This happens because, neurobiologically, they operate in different parts of our brain. Angry moments, unmet expectations, trauma, and hard conversations affect us. Our body responds and keeps score. Ever had an argument? Why is it the next day I think of my best comebacks? That is part of our wiring! How our brains are wired changes based on how we attend to ourselves. What we do and do not do every day impacts how we perform, how we show up, and how we connect to those around us.

Let's consider what happens when we are in an argument. In the moment of the argument, our brain's working memory is in fight/flee mode. Downshifting into fight/flee happens as fast as seven seconds! Sometimes days *after* the argument (depending on the severity), we come up with better, more rational thinking . . . but not always in the moment.

We say we want to be vulnerable, but vulnerability does not come easy for most people. We want to know we are not alone in the struggle, that we can find our way through adversity toward solutions. None of us wants to stay stuck! I believe that!

What this book is about are both the struggle and the gift of processing toward solutions. The process is never-ending. The process is about humility, courage, and doing the next right thing. The process is our journey as educators, parents, and people. I believe that process starts with gratitude.

Did you know that if you keep a gratitude journal over six weeks, you will see at least 25 percent increase in your productivity, performance, and happiness?[1] (Achor, 2017). Gratitude,

My Story

like anything we focus on, alerts our reticular activating system—what we pay attention to grows. Where our attention goes, the energy goes and flows! The science and facts on how our brains operate just give us more evidence for being intentional about our thoughts and words.

Gratitude is essential because if you are like me, you have taken *a lot* for granted.

What do I mean by that?

Well, stop for a second. . . . You are breathing, you have shelter, you have warmth or cool air around you. Maybe you have a college degree, a job you love. Maybe you are reading this on a computer. You have lighting, a window to the outside world. You have freedom. You live in a democracy. There might be sun or rain or snow outside, but life is happening. Things are alive and moving. How we respond to these realities shapes our wiring and our brain chemistry.

Please hear this fact: gratitude is *not* natural. And I'm not suggesting here that you just be "happy." That's crap. Happiness is a product of gratitude and sustainable only through practice and effort. Neurobiologically, in fact, we are hardwired for anger, fear, disgust, sadness, joy, and surprise . . . but not optimism, gratitude, kindness, humility[2] (Ekman, 2011). Those habits are *learned* and traceable every day when we direct attention to them.

Gratitude doesn't mean we settle; it means we grow into being with a new perspective. We can only assist others and be of maximum service to others when our own cup is full. Yes, look for more, but first see what you have from a grateful heart.

Again, this is part of my daily action plan. It's not that I do it perfectly by any means, but it's a process, a journey. It provides me clear direction and action, and it fuels a sense of calm, clear thinking, and my True North.

Unless we have solid boundaries and a sense of who we are at our core, we will get run over by other people's agendas and life's demands. Don't wait for a crisis or make your health someone else's problem. We have to remember we have a choice to keep well-being central to our lives.

My "5 to Thrive" action plan:

1. Gratitude: I create a gratitude list every day—five items minimum. This is why I created this tool to share with you. I want to form a community doing gratitude together. Some examples from my day today: feeling at ease in my own skin, being completely present with my kids, walking outside, time with my husband for a lunch date, the summer breeze, and fresh air. Please note: Either decide to do the gratitude or let it go. If you do let it go, pick up one of the other "5 to Thrive." Doing too much creates hurry. Hurry and indecision are gratitude killers. They just ruin any form of peace because we aren't meant to be "human doings," but "human beings."

2. Food plan: Nutrition means taking time to meet with a nutritionist. Get input from an outside source. Food is healing when used for fuel. I never understood how to eat (with exercise/without it) until I got a plan of eating from a professional. When she asked me, "How may cruciferous vegetables do you eat per day?" I knew I was in trouble! I literally thought: *I have a doctorate and a master's degree; how do I not know how to do this? Is she talking a foreign language?* It is okay to get outside help on any issue from a professional.

3. Centering Prayer: Stop and be still. When faced with distress, stop and pause. Breathe. Ask for guidance. Pray. Slow down enough to process the situation, feeling, or circumstance. My centering prayer fellowship is open to anyone and is twelve-step friendly. Check out 12stepspirituality.org for free access to a library of amazing speakers and talks. In my experience, the move away from our friends and family devastated me. I learned that you cannot replicate decades of friendships in one year. Value your communities! Consider:
- Which communities do you *love* being a part of?

My Story

- Which ones need boundaries?
- In which groups do you feel loved?
- Into which ones do you want to invest more?

My twelve-step fellowship is a buffer to knowing I'm not alone. Other people just like me have been on the journey, and I can gain from their experience strength and hope. My closest inner circle of friends and recovery community are *everything* to me! Being known, feeling a sense of belonging? Uh, there's nothing like it. It's like the old TV show, *Cheers!* " . . . Sometimes you want to go where everybody knows your name, and they are always glad you came." See, I had "friends" before but it was always motivated by conditions. When there are no strings attached, that is a freeing relationship. Our brains enjoy it like nothing else when we are in a joyful feeling with a sense of belonging, trust, and safety. We all benefit from people in life who are "God with skin." They show it through unconditional love and acceptance.

4. Believe every behavior is rooted in a belief about something: When you or I get stuck, beliefs are a great place to start to create self-awareness. What lie are you believing about yourself? Who put that idea into your mind? What can you replace it with? This is important work. Believe in hope. The definition of *hope* means confident expectation for something good to happen. Meaning, I believe gratitude leads to love. I decide to love—love myself and others. Why? Because *what we say in our heads drops down into our hearts*. The body keeps score and runs through those neural pathways into every cell in our bodies. Ask yourself: What are you believing about you, your life, the future?

Do I believe my best work is ahead of me? I have a sign posted with this question in front of my desk. It reminds me—yes, I do! And to stay in today, optimistic.

5. Drink more water and move your body more: Enough said.

My challenge to you:
Use this book! Start. Begin. Yes, you can!
Keep a gratitude journal for five days; then check in with yourself. Was it worth it?
What did you notice?
What happened?
Do you feel differently?
Now, level it up and go for it for five weeks.
What do you observe about the process?
What benefits are you experiencing?
What positives are there to this process?
Whom can you take with you on the journey?

Next up: Get your students involved over 180 days and watch the magic take place in front of you as you do the work independently. I did a process called "Thankful Thursday," in which high school students wrote letters of thanks every single week for the entire school year. I had postage donated and stationery, too. Some kids had never written a letter and didn't know where the stamp went, but they learned how to do it. It became a huge success and full of positive energy, especially when certain people wrote them back. We had more than a thousand thank-you letters last year. During the pandemic, my own kids wrote thank-you letters, and guess what? Each thank you, each letter was a gift for the recipient and my own child.

Your turn:
Start with yourself. You cannot pass on what you don't take on yourself. Do I dream about this at every high school in America? The world? You bet I do. What if we are creating a global movement of thanks . . . one letter at a time? Right now, I can start with my own hula hoop of influence. So can you!

Remember the definition of gratitude: the quality of being thankful; readiness to show appreciation and to return kindness.

My Story

"She expressed her gratitude to the committee for their support."

Gratitude means thanks and appreciation. *Gratitude*, which rhymes with *attitude*, comes from the Latin word *gratus*, which means *thankful*. So good!

Lastly, remember: being thankful is unlike indebtedness,; you're not anxious about having to pay it back.

Have fun as you begin your gratitude journey!

Footnotes:

[1] Schawbel, Don. October 9, 2013, "Shawn Achor: What You Need to Do Before Experiencing Happiness," *Forbes*, November 21, 2017.

[2] Ekman, Paul, *Emotional Revealed: Recognizing Faces and Feelings to Improve Communication and Emotional Life*. New York: Henry Holt, 2007.

My ABC's of Gratitude

Let's begin!

I am grateful for the alphabet! I'll share one word for each letter to get our minds ready and primed for gratitude:

A is for allowing
B is for being
C is for creating
D is for dreaming
E is for engaging
F is for feeling
G is for grounding (in my gut)
H is for Henry (our son)
I is for intuition
J is for Jenifer (me)
K is for kaleidoscope
L is for Lucy (our daughter)
M is for moon
N is for normal
O is for open
P is for permission
Q is for query
R is for respect
S is for sunshine
T is for Todd (my husband)
U is for understanding
V is for vision
W is for wishes
X is for xylophone
Y is for yellow
Z is for Zoey (our daughter)

Self-Reflection Journal:

180 Days of Thank-You's and Often-Overlooked Blessings

Self-Reflection Journal

Day 1

Today's date: _____

"A teacher affects eternity. You can never tell where his influence stops."
– Henry Brooks Adams, American historian

An often-overlooked blessing: Deep breaths.

Today I am looking forward to . . .

1. _____
2. _____
3. _____
4. _____
5. _____

Today I am grateful for . . .

1. _____
2. _____
3. _____
4. _____
5. _____

Day 2

Today's date: _____

*"This is a wonderful day;
I've never seen this one before."*
– Maya Angelou, poet

Thank you for when I rise.

Today I am looking forward to . . .

1. _____
2. _____
3. _____
4. _____
5. _____

Today I am grateful for . . .

1. _____
2. _____
3. _____
4. _____
5. _____

Self-Reflection Journal

Day 3

Today's date: _____

"Feeling gratitude is like opening a present."
– Lucille Baker, Jenny's grandmother

An often-overlooked blessing: Fresh flowers.

Today I am looking forward to . . .

1. _____
2. _____
3. _____
4. _____
5. _____

Today I am grateful for . . .

1. _____
2. _____
3. _____
4. _____
5. _____

Day 4

Today's date: _____

"A good night's sleep is worth loads of joy in the morning."
– **Jim Severson**, Jenny's dad

Thank you for when I rest.

Today I am looking forward to . . .

1. _____
2. _____
3. _____
4. _____
5. _____

Today I am grateful for . . .

1. _____
2. _____
3. _____
4. _____
5. _____

Self-Reflection Journal

Day 5

Today's date: _____

"Gratitude is the fairest blossom that springs from the soul."
– Henry Ward Beecher, author

An often-overlooked blessing: Deep joy for others.

Today I am looking forward to . . .

1. _____
2. _____
3. _____
4. _____
5. _____

Today I am grateful for . . .

1. _____
2. _____
3. _____
4. _____
5. _____

Day 6

Today's date: _____

"The more you praise and celebrate your life, the more there is in life to celebrate."
– **Oprah Winfrey,** OWN network, TV icon

Thank you for feeling the presence of peace.

Today I am looking forward to . . .

1. _____
2. _____
3. _____
4. _____
5. _____

Today I am grateful for . . .

1. _____
2. _____
3. _____
4. _____
5. _____

Self-Reflection Journal

Day 7

Today's date: _____

*"You are only one thought away
from a good feeling."*
– Sheila Krystal, a mother

An often-overlooked blessing: Not having to cook tonight.

Today I am looking forward to . . .

1. _____
2. _____
3. _____
4. _____
5. _____

Today I am grateful for . . .

1. _____
2. _____
3. _____
4. _____
5. _____

Day 8

Today's date: _____

*"It's not what we have in our life,
but who we have in our life that counts."*
– J. M. Laurence, author

Thank you for moments when hope is restored.

Today I am looking forward to . . .

1. _____
2. _____
3. _____
4. _____
5. _____

Today I am grateful for . . .

1. _____
2. _____
3. _____
4. _____
5. _____

Self-Reflection Journal

Day 9

Today's date: _____

"*Life isn't a matter of milestones but of moments.*"
— **Rose Kennedy**, author

An often-overlooked blessing: Answered prayers.

Today I am looking forward to . . .

1. _____
2. _____
3. _____
4. _____
5. _____

Today I am grateful for . . .

1. _____
2. _____
3. _____
4. _____
5. _____

Day 10

Today's date: _____

"I am grateful for whatever helps my spirit grow."
– Florida Calloway, poet

Thank you for the kindness of strangers.

Today I am looking forward to . . .

1. _____
2. _____
3. _____
4. _____
5. _____

Today I am grateful for . . .

1. _____
2. _____
3. _____
4. _____
5. _____

Self-Reflection Journal

Day 11

Today's date: _____

"We can only be said to be alive in those moments when our hearts are conscious of our treasures."
— **Thornton Wilder,** playwright, teacher

An often over-looked blessing: Meeting a person and finding common ground, agreement, humor.

Today I am looking forward to . . .

1. _____
2. _____
3. _____
4. _____
5. _____

Today I am grateful for . . .

1. _____
2. _____
3. _____
4. _____
5. _____

Day 12

Today's date: _____

"All the great blessings of my life are present in my thoughts today."
– **Phoebe Cary**, cancer survivor, advocate

Thank you for the reality or memory of holding your child in your arms.

Today I am looking forward to . . .

1. _____
2. _____
3. _____
4. _____
5. _____

Today I am grateful for . . .

1. _____
2. _____
3. _____
4. _____
5. _____

Self-Reflection Journal

Day 13

Today's date: _____

*"And life is what we make it.
Always has been, always will be."*
— **Charle Fern,** Lake Forest College basketball coach

An often-overlooked blessing: Everyone enjoying the same show.

Today I am looking forward to . . .

1. _____
2. _____
3. _____
4. _____
5. _____

Today I am grateful for . . .

1. _____
2. _____
3. _____
4. _____
5. _____

Day 14

Today's date: _____

"Look for the good and you will always find it."
– Anne Perry, speaker

Thank you for a steady job that allows you to also pursue your dreams (aka side hustle).

Today I am looking forward to . . .

1. _____
2. _____
3. _____
4. _____
5. _____

Today I am grateful for . . .

1. _____
2. _____
3. _____
4. _____
5. _____

Self-Reflection Journal

Day 15

Today's date: _____

"Once we discover how to appreciate the timeless values in our daily experiences, we can enjoy the best things in life."
– **Jerome K. Jerome,** writer, teacher

An often-overlooked blessing: The smell and taste of saltwater.

Today I am looking forward to . . .

1. _____
2. _____
3. _____
4. _____
5. _____

Today I am grateful for . . .

1. _____
2. _____
3. _____
4. _____
5. _____

Day 16

Today's date: _____

""Listen to your own heart. Listen to your own longing. We are all seeking a life that matters."
— **Jon Kabat-Zinn,** philosopher

Thank you for the gift of listening for greatness. What mindfulness is saying to all of us is, find your own way.

Today I am looking forward to . . .

1. _____
2. _____
3. _____
4. _____
5. _____

Today I am grateful for . . .

1. _____
2. _____
3. _____
4. _____
5. _____

Self-Reflection Journal

Day 17

Today's date: _____

"The secret of genius is to carry the spirit of the child into old age."
– **Aldous Huxley,** English novelist

*An often-overlooked blessing:
The precious giggles and laughter of a child.*

Today I am looking forward to . . .

1. _____
2. _____
3. _____
4. _____
5. _____

Today I am grateful for . . .

1. _____
2. _____
3. _____
4. _____
5. _____

Day 18

Today's date: _____

"Standing in the middle of the road is very dangerous; you get knocked down by traffic."
– **Margaret Thatcher,** UK prime minister

Thank you for the freedom to vote.

Today I am looking forward to . . .

1. _____
2. _____
3. _____
4. _____
5. _____

Today I am grateful for . . .

1. _____
2. _____
3. _____
4. _____
5. _____

Self-Reflection Journal

Day 19

Today's date: _____

"Little flower, but if I could understand what you are, root and all, I would know what a God and [woman] is."
— **Alfred, Lord Tennyson,** English poet

An often-overlooked blessing: Cherry blossoms.

Today I am looking forward to . . .

1. _____
2. _____
3. _____
4. _____
5. _____

Today I am grateful for . . .

1. _____
2. _____
3. _____
4. _____
5. _____

Day 20

Today's date: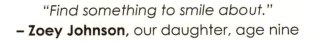

"Find something to smile about."
– Zoey Johnson, our daughter, age nine

Thank you for replotting; giving yourself room to grow.

Today I am looking forward to . . .

1. _____
2. _____
3. _____
4. _____
5. _____

Today I am grateful for . . .

1. _____
2. _____
3. _____
4. _____
5. _____

Self-Reflection Journal

Day 21

Today's date: _____

"We must always be on the lookout for the presence of wonder."
– **E. B. White,** American essayist

An often-overlooked blessing: The lakes, ocean, and blue sea.

Today I am looking forward to . . .

1. _____
2. _____
3. _____
4. _____
5. _____

Today I am grateful for . . .

1. _____
2. _____
3. _____
4. _____
5. _____

Day 22

Today's date: _____

"There are far, far better things ahead than any we leave behind."
– C. S. Lewis, scholar, novelist

Thank you for the texture of a quality rug.

Today I am looking forward to . . .

1. _____
2. _____
3. _____
4. _____
5. _____

Today I am grateful for . . .

1. _____
2. _____
3. _____
4. _____
5. _____

Self-Reflection Journal

Day 23

Today's date: _____

"If you have good thoughts, they will shine out of your face like sunbeams, and you will always look lovely."
— **Roald Dahl,** author, inventor

An often-overlooked blessing: Bright sunshine after a storm.

Today I am looking forward to . . .

1. _____
2. _____
3. _____
4. _____
5. _____

Today I am grateful for . . .

1. _____
2. _____
3. _____
4. _____
5. _____

Day 24

Today's date: _____

"There is something in every season in every day to celebrate with thanksgiving."
– Gloria Gaither, songwriter

Thank you for deep colors of red, green, and blue.

Today I am looking forward to . . .

1. _____
2. _____
3. _____
4. _____
5. _____

Today I am grateful for . . .

1. _____
2. _____
3. _____
4. _____
5. _____

Self-Reflection Journal

Day 25

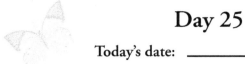

Today's date: _____

"Let us be grateful to people who make us happy."
— **Marcel Proust,** French novelist

Thank you for the overlooked blessing of simple mistakes, grace and the reminder to err is human, to allow grace is divine.

Today I am looking forward to . . .

1. _____
2. _____
3. _____
4. _____
5. _____

Today I am grateful for . . .

1. _____
2. _____
3. _____
4. _____
5. _____

The Educator's 180-Day Gratitude Turnaround

Day 26

Today's date: _____

"We must find time to stop and thank the people who make a difference in our lives."
– John F. Kennedy, thirty-fifth American president

An often-overlooked blessing: Familiar faces and friends.

Today I am looking forward to . . .

1. _____
2. _____
3. _____
4. _____
5. _____

Today I am grateful for . . .

1. _____
2. _____
3. _____
4. _____
5. _____

Self-Reflection Journal

Day 27

Today's date: _____

"A wise man loses nothing if he but save himself."
– **Michel de Montaigne,** French philosopher

Thank you for vision boards to map out dreams.

Today I am looking forward to . . .

1. _____
2. _____
3. _____
4. _____
5. _____

Today I am grateful for . . .

1. _____
2. _____
3. _____
4. _____
5. _____

Day 28

Today's date: _____

"Live in the sunshine. Swim in the sea. Drink the wild air."
– Ralph Waldo Emerson,
American essayist, lecturer, poet

An often-overlooked blessing:
Technology to connect us, our devices, computers.

Today I am looking forward to . . .

1. _____
2. _____
3. _____
4. _____
5. _____

Today I am grateful for . . .

1. _____
2. _____
3. _____
4. _____
5. _____

Self-Reflection Journal

Day 29

Today's date: _____

"Have a heart that never hardens, and a temper that never tires and a touch that never hurts."
– Charles Dickens, British novelist

Thank you for fuzzy blankets.

Today I am looking forward to . . .

1. _____
2. _____
3. _____
4. _____
5. _____

Today I am grateful for . . .

1. _____
2. _____
3. _____
4. _____
5. _____

Day 30

Today's date: _____

"Have patience with everything unresolved in your heart."
– **Rainer Maria Rilke,** German poet

An often-overlooked blessing: The beach breeze and sand between my toes.

Today I am looking forward to . . .

1. _____
2. _____
3. _____
4. _____
5. _____

Today I am grateful for . . .

1. _____
2. _____
3. _____
4. _____
5. _____

Self-Reflection Journal

Day 31

Today's date: _____

"I took a deep breath and listened to the old bray of my heart. I am. I am. I am."
— **Sylvia Plath,** American poet

Thank you for words of affirmation after doing a great job and having your efforts appreciated and respected.

Today I am looking forward to . . .

1. _____
2. _____
3. _____
4. _____
5. _____

Today I am grateful for . . .

1. _____
2. _____
3. _____
4. _____
5. _____

Day 32

Today's date: _____

"I knew who I was this morning, but I've changed a few times since then."
— **Lewis Carroll,** British author

An often-overlooked blessing: Trying something new and loving it!

Today I am looking forward to . . .

1. _____
2. _____
3. _____
4. _____
5. _____

Today I am grateful for . . .

1. _____
2. _____
3. _____
4. _____
5. _____

Self-Reflection Journal

Day 33

Today's date: _____

"There is not always a good guy, nor is there always a bad guy; most people are somewhere in between."
– **Patrick Ness,** British author

Thank you for a nap.

Today I am looking forward to . . .

1. _____
2. _____
3. _____
4. _____
5. _____

Today I am grateful for . . .

1. _____
2. _____
3. _____
4. _____
5. _____

The Educator's 180-Day Gratitude Turnaround

Day 34

Today's date: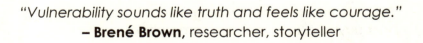

"Vulnerability sounds like truth and feels like courage."
– Brené Brown, researcher, storyteller

An often-overlooked blessing: The sacred release of a good cry.

Today I am looking forward to . . .

1. _____
2. _____
3. _____
4. _____
5. _____

Today I am grateful for . . .

1. _____
2. _____
3. _____
4. _____
5. _____

Self-Reflection Journal

Day 35

Today's date: _____

"Be patient and be tough. Someday this pain will be useful to you."
— **Ovid**, Roman poet

Thank you for the gift of receiving flowers.

Today I am looking forward to . . .

1. _____
2. _____
3. _____
4. _____
5. _____

Today I am grateful for . . .

1. _____
2. _____
3. _____
4. _____
5. _____

Day 36

Today's date: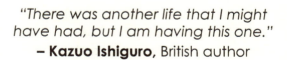

"There was another life that I might have had, but I am having this one."
— **Kazuo Ishiguro,** British author

An often-overlooked blessing: Moving on.

Today I am looking forward to . . .

1. _____
2. _____
3. _____
4. _____
5. _____

Today I am grateful for . . .

1. _____
2. _____
3. _____
4. _____
5. _____

Self-Reflection Journal

Day 37

Today's date: _____

"This above all: to thine own self be true."
– William Shakespeare, playwright, actor, poet

Often-overlooked blessing: Deep breaths.

Today I am looking forward to . . .

1. _____
2. _____
3. _____
4. _____
5. _____

Today I am grateful for . . .

1. _____
2. _____
3. _____
4. _____
5. _____

Day 38

Today's date: _____

"It is not down on any map; true places never are."
– **Herman Melville**, *Moby Dick* author

An often-overlooked blessing: Feeling a sense of pride in oneself.

Today I am looking forward to . . .

1. _____
2. _____
3. _____
4. _____
5. _____

Today I am grateful for . . .

1. _____
2. _____
3. _____
4. _____
5. _____

Self-Reflection Journal

Day 39

Today's date: _____

"There are always flowers for those who want to see them."
— **Henri Matisse**, French painter

Thank you for meeting a deadline.

Today I am looking forward to . . .

1. _____
2. _____
3. _____
4. _____
5. _____

Today I am grateful for . . .

1. _____
2. _____
3. _____
4. _____
5. _____

Day 40

Today's date: _____

"Deciding to simplify our lives and bring order to our lives by sending objects that we no longer love to new, happier incarnations with people who will genuinely appreciate them is the way to open up to the abundance that will perfectly suit us."
– Sarah Ban Breathnach, author

An often-overlooked blessing: Saying no without guilt.

Today I am looking forward to . . .

1. _____
2. _____
3. _____
4. _____
5. _____

Today I am grateful for . . .

1. _____
2. _____
3. _____
4. _____
5. _____

Self-Reflection Journal

Day 41

Today's date: _____

"There is nothing that can equal the treasure of so many shared memories."
– Antoine de Saint-Exupéry, French writer

Thank you for the gift of recycling; knowing someone will be able to re-use, repurpose items in a variety of forms.

Today I am looking forward to . . .

1. _____
2. _____
3. _____
4. _____
5. _____

Today I am grateful for . . .

1. _____
2. _____
3. _____
4. _____
5. _____

Day 42

Today's date: _____

"Have nothing in your homes that you do not know to be useful and believe to be beautiful."
– **William Morris,** designer

An often-overlooked blessing: Tossing out/donating items that no longer serve you or the space in which you live.

Today I am looking forward to . . .

1. _____
2. _____
3. _____
4. _____
5. _____

Today I am grateful for . . .

1. _____
2. _____
3. _____
4. _____
5. _____

Self-Reflection Journal

Day 43

Today's date: _____

"It was the best of times, it was the worst of times."
– Charles Dickens, novelist

*Thank you for being able to provide for
the needs and wants of our loved ones.*

Today I am looking forward to . . .

1. _____
2. _____
3. _____
4. _____
5. _____

Today I am grateful for . . .

1. _____
2. _____
3. _____
4. _____
5. _____

Day 44

Today's date: _____

"It is only with gratitude that life becomes rich."
– **Dietrich Bonhoeffer**, German theologian

*An often-overlooked blessing:
Reading a book that changes your life.*

Today I am looking forward to . . .

1. _____
2. _____
3. _____
4. _____
5. _____

Today I am grateful for . . .

1. _____
2. _____
3. _____
4. _____
5. _____

Self-Reflection Journal

Day 45

Today's date: _____

*"It is not joy that makes us grateful;
it is gratitude that makes us joyful."*
— David Steindl-Rast, monk, author, lecturer

Thank you for being able to travel.

Today I am looking forward to . . .

1. _____
2. _____
3. _____
4. _____
5. _____

Today I am grateful for . . .

1. _____
2. _____
3. _____
4. _____
5. _____

Day 46

Today's date: _____

"Be grateful for the home you have, knowing that at this moment all you have is all you need."
– Sarah Ban Breathnach, author

An often-overlooked blessing: Finding a parking spot exactly when you need it.

Today I am looking forward to . . .

1. _____
2. _____
3. _____
4. _____
5. _____

Today I am grateful for . . .

1. _____
2. _____
3. _____
4. _____
5. _____

Self-Reflection Journal

Day 47

Today's date: _____

"Some of the most important things in life aren't things."
– Linda Ellerbee, American journalist

Thank you for trust between friends.

Today I am looking forward to . . .

1. _____
2. _____
3. _____
4. _____
5. _____

Today I am grateful for . . .

1. _____
2. _____
3. _____
4. _____
5. _____

Day 48

Today's date: _____

"Light tomorrow with today."
– Elizabeth Barrett Browning, English poet

An often-overlooked blessing: Starting where you are.

Today I am looking forward to . . .

1. _____
2. _____
3. _____
4. _____
5. _____

Today I am grateful for . . .

1. _____
2. _____
3. _____
4. _____
5. _____

Self-Reflection Journal

Day 49

Today's date: _____

"Treasure this day and treasure yourself truly; neither will ever happen again."
— **Ray Bradbury,** novelist

Thank you for the long-awaited call with good news.

Today I am looking forward to . . .

1. _____
2. _____
3. _____
4. _____
5. _____

Today I am grateful for . . .

1. _____
2. _____
3. _____
4. _____
5. _____

Day 50

Today's date: _____

"Where so many hours have been spent in convincing myself that I am right, is there not some reason to fear I may be wrong?"
 – Jane Austen, English novelist

An often-overlooked blessing: Your favorite mentor.

Today I am looking forward to . . .

1. _____
2. _____
3. _____
4. _____
5. _____

Today I am grateful for . . .

1. _____
2. _____
3. _____
4. _____
5. _____

Self-Reflection Journal

Day 51

Today's date: _____

"I believe the nicest and sweetest days are not those on which anything very splendid or wonderful or exciting happens, but just those that bring simple little pleasure following one another softly, like pearls slipping off a string."
– Lucy Maud Montgomery, Canadian author

An often-overlooked blessing:
The fresh smell of a new box of crayons.

Today I am looking forward to . . .

1. _____
2. _____
3. _____
4. _____
5. _____

Today I am grateful for . . .

1. _____
2. _____
3. _____
4. _____
5. _____

Day 52

Today's date: _____

"I'd rather have roses on my table than diamonds on my neck."
– Emma Goldman, anarchist, author

An often-overlooked blessing: Reawakened ideas and passions; letting go of old habits.

Today I am looking forward to . . .

1. _____
2. _____
3. _____
4. _____
5. _____

Today I am grateful for . . .

1. _____
2. _____
3. _____
4. _____
5. _____

Self-Reflection Journal

Day 53

Today's date: _____

"Joy is what happens to us when we allow ourselves to recognize how good things really are."
– **Marianne Williamson,** author

Thank you for when the repair bill is less than you expected.

Today I am looking forward to . . .

1. _____
2. _____
3. _____
4. _____
5. _____

Today I am grateful for . . .

1. _____
2. _____
3. _____
4. _____
5. _____

Day 54

Today's date: _____

"Plant it with the green side up."
– Mary Ann and Frederick McGourty, gardeners

An often-overlooked blessing: A hard rainstorm.

Today I am looking forward to . . .

1. _____
2. _____
3. _____
4. _____
5. _____

Today I am grateful for . . .

1. _____
2. _____
3. _____
4. _____
5. _____

Self-Reflection Journal

Day 55

Today's date: _____

"Grace fills empty spaces, but it can only enter where there is a void to receive it, and it is grace itself which makes this void."
– Simone Weil, French philosopher

Thank you for the first snowfall of the season.

Today I am looking forward to . . .

1. _____
2. _____
3. _____
4. _____
5. _____

Today I am grateful for . . .

1. _____
2. _____
3. _____
4. _____
5. _____

Day 56

Today's date: _____

"Let your mind be quiet, realizing the beauty of the world, and the immense, boundless treasures that it holds in store."
– **Edward Carpenter,** English poet

An often-overlooked blessing: The ever-changing seasons, fall, winter, spring; the newness of each passing day marked by seasons.

Today I am looking forward to . . .

1. _____
2. _____
3. _____
4. _____
5. _____

Today I am grateful for . . .

1. _____
2. _____
3. _____
4. _____
5. _____

Self-Reflection Journal

Day 57

Today's date: _____

"I have a number of different callings. And I think it's possible to be called away from things I have been called to in the past. There are goodbyes as well as hellos in our callings. Because a calling doesn't have to be for a lifetime."
– **Barbara Brown Taylor,** Episcopal priest, theologian

Thank you for the miracle cure of a hot bath or sauna.

Today I am looking forward to . . .

1. _____
2. _____
3. _____
4. _____
5. _____

Today I am grateful for . . .

1. _____
2. _____
3. _____
4. _____
5. _____

Day 58

Today's date: _____

"My life will always have dirty dishes. If this sink can become a place of contemplation, let me learn constancy here."
– Gunilla Norris, writer, meditation teacher

An often-overlooked blessing:
The ability to laugh in tense situations.

Today I am looking forward to . . .

1. _____
2. _____
3. _____
4. _____
5. _____

Today I am grateful for . . .

1. _____
2. _____
3. _____
4. _____
5. _____

Self-Reflection Journal

Day 59

Today's date: _____

"The grass is always greener where you water it."
– Author unknown

Thank you for the perspective to see humor in ourselves.

Today I am looking forward to . . .

1. _____
2. _____
3. _____
4. _____
5. _____

Today I am grateful for . . .

1. _____
2. _____
3. _____
4. _____
5. _____

The Educator's 180-Day Gratitude Turnaround

Day 60

Today's date: _____

"Write your top-ten list of things I love about my kids, print them out and put them on their breakfast plates, or in lunch boxes, stand back and smile."
– Mandy Arioto, president, MOPS International

An often-overlooked blessing: Healthy children.

Today I am looking forward to . . .

1. _____
2. _____
3. _____
4. _____
5. _____

Today I am grateful for . . .

1. _____
2. _____
3. _____
4. _____
5. _____

Self-Reflection Journal

Day 61

Today's date: _____

"If you're rested, if your mind is in peace and if you're full of love and compassion, if you come from being and then feeling, and then self-reflection, then things will with synchronicity fall into place. That's how nature functions. Like the seed. In every seed is the promise of thousands of forests."
– Deepak Chopra, author

Thank you for the wisdom of great teachers.

Today I am looking forward to . . .

1. _____
2. _____
3. _____
4. _____
5. _____

Today I am grateful for . . .

1. _____
2. _____
3. _____
4. _____
5. _____

Day 62

Today's date: _____

"The soul is the lure of our becoming. We are coded in our cells. We are coded in our hearts. We are in our becoming. And we are God's seeds, becoming God's selves."
– Jean Houston, American author

An often-overlooked blessing: Sharing your aspirations for the future with a dear friend, and hearing their encouragement and advice.

Today I am looking forward to . . .

1. _____
2. _____
3. _____
4. _____
5. _____

Today I am grateful for . . .

1. _____
2. _____
3. _____
4. _____
5. _____

Self-Reflection Journal

Day 63

Today's date: _____

"Love created this space for me once I became open to allowing it in my life."
– Julia Cameron, author and filmmaker

Thank you for the sound of raindrops on your roof at night.

Today I am looking forward to . . .

1. _____
2. _____
3. _____
4. _____
5. _____

Today I am grateful for . . .

1. _____
2. _____
3. _____
4. _____
5. _____

The Educator's 180-Day Gratitude Turnaround

Day 64

Today's date: _____

"Do not think it will work for others and not you; today be open to allowing a creative, sacred space to come into your world."
– Joan Borysenko, Ph.D., medical scientist

An often-overlooked blessing: An unexpected compliment that makes your day.

Today I am looking forward to . . .

1. _____
2. _____
3. _____
4. _____
5. _____

Today I am grateful for . . .

1. _____
2. _____
3. _____
4. _____
5. _____

Self-Reflection Journal

Day 65

Today's date: _____

"Love is the answer."
– Rob Bell, American author

Thank you for an outdoor wedding on a lovely day.

Today I am looking forward to . . .

1. _____
2. _____
3. _____
4. _____
5. _____

Today I am grateful for . . .

1. _____
2. _____
3. _____
4. _____
5. _____

The Educator's 180-Day Gratitude Turnaround

Day 66

Today's date: _____

"You can, you should, and if you're brave enough to start, you will."
— **Stephen King**, author

An often-overlooked blessing: Paying off your credit card balance.

Today I am looking forward to . . .

1. _____
2. _____
3. _____
4. _____
5. _____

Today I am grateful for . . .

1. _____
2. _____
3. _____
4. _____
5. _____

Self-Reflection Journal

Day 67

Today's date: _____

"You must have a room or a certain hour of the day or so where you do not know what was in the morning paper . . . a place where you can simply experience and bring forth what you are, and what you might be . . . at first you may find nothing's happening . . . but if you have a sacred place and use it, take advantage of it, something will happen."
– **Joseph Campbell**, American author

Thank you for a day of rest.

Today I am looking forward to . . .

1. _____
2. _____
3. _____
4. _____
5. _____

Today I am grateful for . . .

1. _____
2. _____
3. _____
4. _____
5. _____

Day 68

Today's date: _____

"Just because you hear crickets, doesn't mean no one is listening."
– Jess Ekstrom, author, speaker

An often-overlooked blessing: Running into an old friend.

Today I am looking forward to . . .

1. _____
2. _____
3. _____
4. _____
5. _____

Today I am grateful for . . .

1. _____
2. _____
3. _____
4. _____
5. _____

Self-Reflection Journal

Day 69

Today's date: _____

"Getting turned on to a joy-packed lifestyle is the power of positive living, and the feeling of peace inside and the joy of forgiveness—this is what I want to share with you."
– Norman Vincent Peale, author

Thank you for breathing a sigh of relief.

Today I am looking forward to . . .

1. _____
2. _____
3. _____
4. _____
5. _____

Today I am grateful for . . .

1. _____
2. _____
3. _____
4. _____
5. _____

Day 70

Today's date: _____

"When people portray various emotions, their bodies produce matching physiological patterns such as changes in heart and breathing rates. Simply put, when you act happy, you'll feel happy. And vice versa."
– Paul Ekman, emotion scientist

An often-overlooked blessing: Visiting your hometown decades later with new eyes.

Today I am looking forward to . . .

1. _____
2. _____
3. _____
4. _____
5. _____

Today I am grateful for . . .

1. _____
2. _____
3. _____
4. _____
5. _____

Self-Reflection Journal

Day 71

Today's date: _____

"Just as the butterfly must leave the security of the chrysalis, so must the student leave the 'chrysalis' of the educational setting and rely on their own inner resources."
– Micki McKisson, teacher

Thank you for a home-cooked meal that smells delicious the moment you walk in the door.

Today I am looking forward to . . .

1. _____
2. _____
3. _____
4. _____
5. _____

Today I am grateful for . . .

1. _____
2. _____
3. _____
4. _____
5. _____

Day 72

Today's date: _____

"Neurogenesis is real, and there is no middle ground; you are either moving toward new patterns or away. The choice is yours."
– Eric Jensen, member, Society of Neuroscience

An often-overlooked blessing: Doing the work. The practice of and creation of new habits forming in my mind. My brain is changing for the better and I can feel it! Yes, I can.

Today I am looking forward to . . .

1. _____
2. _____
3. _____
4. _____
5. _____

Today I am grateful for . . .

1. _____
2. _____
3. _____
4. _____
5. _____

Self-Reflection Journal

Day 73

Today's date: _____

"Everyone needs time to think and learn."
– **Grace Pilon,** nun, Sisters of Blessed Sacrament

Thank you for running water and the first glass of the day toward good hydration.

Today I am looking forward to . . .

1. _____
2. _____
3. _____
4. _____
5. _____

Today I am grateful for . . .

1. _____
2. _____
3. _____
4. _____
5. _____

The Educator's 180-Day Gratitude Turnaround

Day 74

Today's date: _____

"Nothing in the world can take the place of persistence. Talent will not; nothing is more common than unsuccessful men with talent. Genius will not; the world is full of educated derelicts. The slogan 'press on' has solved and always will solve the problems of the human race."
– **Calvin Coolidge**, thirtieth U.S. president

An often-overlooked blessing:
Helpful friends and moms who do life together.

Today I am looking forward to . . .

1. _____
2. _____
3. _____
4. _____
5. _____

Today I am grateful for . . .

1. _____
2. _____
3. _____
4. _____
5. _____

Self-Reflection Journal

Day 75

Today's date: _____

*"Be confident, for the stars are
of the same stuff as you."*
– Nikolaj Velimirovic, monk

*Thank you for my desk, my classroom spaces,
and the school in which I am privileged to work.*

Today I am looking forward to . . .

1. _____
2. _____
3. _____
4. _____
5. _____

Today I am grateful for . . .

1. _____
2. _____
3. _____
4. _____
5. _____

Day 76

Today's date: _____

"They are able because they think they are able."
— **Virgil,** Roman poet

An often-overlooked blessing: Heat, the sunshine, and the way the trees move and sway.

Today I am looking forward to . . .

1. _____
2. _____
3. _____
4. _____
5. _____

Today I am grateful for . . .

1. _____
2. _____
3. _____
4. _____
5. _____

Self-Reflection Journal

Day 77

Today's date: _____

*"We should not only use the brains
we have, but all that we can borrow."*
– Woodrow Wilson, twenty-eighth U.S. president

*Thank you for creating a space and place
that feels welcoming to all who enter.*

Today I am looking forward to . . .

1. _____
2. _____
3. _____
4. _____
5. _____

Today I am grateful for . . .

1. _____
2. _____
3. _____
4. _____
5. _____

The Educator's 180-Day Gratitude Turnaround

Day 78

Today's date: _____

"I lose all my good inspiration when my parents are disappointed with me or I get a bad grade in school."
— **Beth,** high school student

An often-overlooked blessing: Ability to express my gratitude in silence, as well as written and verbal forms.

Today I am looking forward to . . .

1. _____
2. _____
3. _____
4. _____
5. _____

Today I am grateful for . . .

1. _____
2. _____
3. _____
4. _____
5. _____

Self-Reflection Journal

Day 79

Today's date: _____

"It takes a whole village to raise a child."
– African proverb

Thank you for blue skies today, and no matter what the weather is outside, I can create sunshine and good light energy in my own being.

Today I am looking forward to . . .

1. _____
2. _____
3. _____
4. _____
5. _____

Today I am grateful for . . .

1. _____
2. _____
3. _____
4. _____
5. _____

Day 80

Today's date: _____

"Fall seven times, stand up eight."
– Japanese proverb

An often-overlooked blessing:
The smell of crayons in a new package.

Today I am looking forward to . . .

1. _____
2. _____
3. _____
4. _____
5. _____

Today I am grateful for . . .

1. _____
2. _____
3. _____
4. _____
5. _____

Self-Reflection Journal

Day 81

Today's date: _____

"If you can read this, thank a teacher."
– bumper sticker

Thank you for how the brain is rewired and reconnected.

Today I am looking forward to . . .

1. _____
2. _____
3. _____
4. _____
5. _____

Today I am grateful for . . .

1. _____
2. _____
3. _____
4. _____
5. _____

Day 82

Today's date: _____

"Give up sainthood, renounce wisdom, and it will be a hundred times better for everyone."
– Lao Tzu, Chinese philosopher

*An often-overlooked blessing:
A night alone to reflect, write, and read.*

Today I am looking forward to . . .

1. _____
2. _____
3. _____
4. _____
5. _____

Today I am grateful for . . .

1. _____
2. _____
3. _____
4. _____
5. _____

Self-Reflection Journal

Day 83

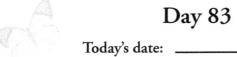

Today's date: _____

"Pity the poor teacher who is not surpassed by his students."
– Anonymous

Thank you for all the teachers who have helped me along the way.

Today I am looking forward to . . .

1. _____
2. _____
3. _____
4. _____
5. _____

Today I am grateful for . . .

1. _____
2. _____
3. _____
4. _____
5. _____

Day 84

Today's date: _____

"The greater a man is, the more distasteful is praise and flattery to him."
– John Burrough, American naturalist

An often-overlooked blessing: The power of being present to exactly where you are.

Today I am looking forward to . . .

1. _____
2. _____
3. _____
4. _____
5. _____

Today I am grateful for . . .

1. _____
2. _____
3. _____
4. _____
5. _____

Self-Reflection Journal

Day 85

Today's date: _____

"An endeavor to please elders is at the bottom of high marks and mediocre careers."
– **John Chapman,** eccentric frontier nurseryman

Thank you for treasured friends with whom you don't miss a beat after some time away.

Today I am looking forward to . . .

1. _____
2. _____
3. _____
4. _____
5. _____

Today I am grateful for . . .

1. _____
2. _____
3. _____
4. _____
5. _____

The Educator's 180-Day Gratitude Turnaround

Day 86

Today's date: _____

"There is no possible method of compelling a child to feel sympathy or affection."
– Bertrand Russell, British philosopher

An often-overlooked blessing: Asking oneself, "Does your whole body say yes?"

Today I am looking forward to . . .

1. _____
2. _____
3. _____
4. _____
5. _____

Today I am grateful for . . .

1. _____
2. _____
3. _____
4. _____
5. _____

Self-Reflection Journal

Day 87

Today's date: _____

"Consider the postage stamp: its usefulness consists in the ability to stick to one thing till it gets there."
– **Josh Billings,** American humorist

*Thank you for endurance to run
the race and margin to slow down.*

Today I am looking forward to . . .

1. _____
2. _____
3. _____
4. _____
5. _____

Today I am grateful for . . .

1. _____
2. _____
3. _____
4. _____
5. _____

Day 88

Today's date: _____

"Do you realize if it weren't for Edison, we'd be watching TV by candlelight?"
– Al Boliska, Toronto radio personality

An often-overlooked blessing: Being able to say, "Hell, yes," and "Hell, no."

Today I am looking forward to . . .

1. _____
2. _____
3. _____
4. _____
5. _____

Today I am grateful for . . .

1. _____
2. _____
3. _____
4. _____
5. _____

Self-Reflection Journal

Day 89

Today's date: _____

"Every individual has a place to fill in the world and is important in some respect, whether he chooses to be so or not."
– **Nathaniel Hawthorne,** American novelist

Thank you for patience and gentleness and self-control.

Today I am looking forward to . . .

1. _____
2. _____
3. _____
4. _____
5. _____

Today I am grateful for . . .

1. _____
2. _____
3. _____
4. _____
5. _____

The Educator's 180-Day Gratitude Turnaround

Day 90

Today's date: _____

"You are in this moment exactly what you are. You do not lack anything, nor is there anything broken or missing. You have all the power and potential you need for further growth."
– **Don Havil**, judge

*An often-overlooked blessing:
Health, wellness, vitality, and strength.*

Today I am looking forward to . . .

1. _____
2. _____
3. _____
4. _____
5. _____

Today I am grateful for . . .

1. _____
2. _____
3. _____
4. _____
5. _____

Self-Reflection Journal

Day 91

Today's date: _____

"Which can say more than this rich praise; that you are not alone."
– William Shakespeare, English playwright

Thank you for transportation to my workplace.

Today I am looking forward to . . .

1. _____
2. _____
3. _____
4. _____
5. _____

Today I am grateful for . . .

1. _____
2. _____
3. _____
4. _____
5. _____

Day 92

Today's date: _____

"When I'm inspired, I jump up and down."
– Henry Johnson, age six

An often-overlooked blessing: The joy of children's laughter and excitement.

Today I am looking forward to . . .

1. _____
2. _____
3. _____
4. _____
5. _____

Today I am grateful for . . .

1. _____
2. _____
3. _____
4. _____
5. _____

Self-Reflection Journal

Day 93

Today's date: _____

"Progress always involves risk. You can't steal second base and keep your foot on first."
– Frederick B. Wilcox, professional footballer

Thank you for food that gives nutrition to the body and energy to thrive.

Today I am looking forward to . . .

1. _____
2. _____
3. _____
4. _____
5. _____

Today I am grateful for . . .

1. _____
2. _____
3. _____
4. _____
5. _____

The Educator's 180-Day Gratitude Turnaround

Day 94

Today's date: _____

"Even in the kindest and gentlest of schools, children are afraid, many of them a great deal of the time, some of them almost all of the time. This is a hard fact to deal with."
– **John Holt,** educator

An often-overlooked blessing:
Courage to say no and set boundaries.

Today I am looking forward to . . .

1. _____
2. _____
3. _____
4. _____
5. _____

Today I am grateful for . . .

1. _____
2. _____
3. _____
4. _____
5. _____

Self-Reflection Journal

Day 95

Today's date: _____

"Use what talents you possess: the woods would be very silent if no birds sang there except those that sang best."
– Henry Van Dyke, Dutch poet

Thank you for the abundant world and birds that soar through the sky.

Today I am looking forward to . . .

1. _____
2. _____
3. _____
4. _____
5. _____

Today I am grateful for . . .

1. _____
2. _____
3. _____
4. _____
5. _____

Day 96

Today's date: _____

"There is only one subject matter for education, and that is life in all its manifestations."
– John Dewey, philosopher, educator

An often-overlooked blessing: That I lack nothing for survival.

Today I am looking forward to . . .

1. _____
2. _____
3. _____
4. _____
5. _____

Today I am grateful for . . .

1. _____
2. _____
3. _____
4. _____
5. _____

Self-Reflection Journal

Day 97

Today's date: _____

"The apple tree never asks the beech how he shall row, nor the lion, the horse, how he shall take his prey."
– William Blake, English poet

Thank you for mended relationships.

Today I am looking forward to . . .

1. _____
2. _____
3. _____
4. _____
5. _____

Today I am grateful for . . .

1. _____
2. _____
3. _____
4. _____
5. _____

Day 98

Today's date: _____

"We can learn something new anytime we believe we can."
– Virginia Satir, American author and therapist

An often-overlooked blessing: Forgiveness—that freeing feeling of letting go of the past. Open to everything ahead with love and joy.

Today I am looking forward to . . .

1. _____
2. _____
3. _____
4. _____
5. _____

Today I am grateful for . . .

1. _____
2. _____
3. _____
4. _____
5. _____

Self-Reflection Journal

Day 99

Today's date: _____

"Human nature is ever capable of improvement and never able of being made perfect."
– **John Clare,** English poet

Thank you for new healthy perspectives.

Today I am looking forward to . . .

1. _____
2. _____
3. _____
4. _____
5. _____

Today I am grateful for . . .

1. _____
2. _____
3. _____
4. _____
5. _____

Day 100

Today's date: _____

*"Learn from the past. Plan for the future.
Live in the present. Rest in the afternoon."*
– Anonymous

Thank you for the kindness of strangers.

Today I am looking forward to . . .

1. _____
2. _____
3. _____
4. _____
5. _____

Today I am grateful for . . .

1. _____
2. _____
3. _____
4. _____
5. _____

Self-Reflection Journal

Day 101

Today's date: _____

"*Attitudes are contagious. Children are extensions of us. When we make teaching come alive, every child wins.*"
— **Jenny Severson,** educator

An often-overlooked blessing: Participation of your students; feeling like you are winning as an educator.

Today I am looking forward to . . .

1. _____
2. _____
3. _____
4. _____
5. _____

Today I am grateful for . . .

1. _____
2. _____
3. _____
4. _____
5. _____

Day 102

Today's date: _____

"Fears are paper tigers."
– Amelia Earhart, American aviator

*Thank you for the crisp autumn
leaves that glisten in the sunshine.*

Today I am looking forward to . . .

1. _____
2. _____
3. _____
4. _____
5. _____

Today I am grateful for . . .

1. _____
2. _____
3. _____
4. _____
5. _____

Self-Reflection Journal

Day 103

Today's date: _____

"The wound is the place where the light enters you."
— **Rumi**, Persian poet

An often-overlooked blessing: When there's a downpour and the rain allows us to pause.

Today I am looking forward to . . .

1. _____
2. _____
3. _____
4. _____
5. _____

Today I am grateful for . . .

1. _____
2. _____
3. _____
4. _____
5. _____

Day 104

Today's date: _____

"Throw your dreams into space like a kite, and you do not know what it will bring back. A new life, a new friend, a new love, a new country."
– **Anais Nin**, French-Cuban essayist

Thank you for the energy and passion to learn, teach, and love one another, and friendships that endure the test of time.

Today I am looking forward to . . .

1. _____
2. _____
3. _____
4. _____
5. _____

Today I am grateful for . . .

1. _____
2. _____
3. _____
4. _____
5. _____

Self-Reflection Journal

Day 105

Today's date: _____

"Explore. Dream. Discover."
– Mark Twain, American writer

An often-overlooked blessing: Taking the long view; not being in a hurry or indecisive.

Today I am looking forward to . . .

1. _____
2. _____
3. _____
4. _____
5. _____

Today I am grateful for . . .

1. _____
2. _____
3. _____
4. _____
5. _____

Day 106

Today's date: _____

"Simplify, simplify."
– Henry David Thoreau, American essayist

Thank you for words of great speakers and talented orators, whose quotes and verses sustain and spark new ideas in me.

Today I am looking forward to . . .

1. _____
2. _____
3. _____
4. _____
5. _____

Today I am grateful for . . .

1. _____
2. _____
3. _____
4. _____
5. _____

Self-Reflection Journal

Day 107

Today's date: _____

"Have patience with everything unresolved in your heart."
– **Rainer Maria Rilke,** German poet

An often-overlooked blessing: Grateful knowing what shame is and how to let it go. (Thanks, Brené Brown!)

Today I am looking forward to . . .

1. _____
2. _____
3. _____
4. _____
5. _____

Today I am grateful for . . .

1. _____
2. _____
3. _____
4. _____
5. _____

Day 108

Today's date: _____

"Courage, dear heart."
– C. S. Lewis, author

Thank you for the happiness that comes from having everything I need today.

Today I am looking forward to . . .

1. _____
2. _____
3. _____
4. _____
5. _____

Today I am grateful for . . .

1. _____
2. _____
3. _____
4. _____
5. _____

Self-Reflection Journal

Day 109

Today's date: _____

"If you want to build a ship, don't drum up people to collect wood and don't assign them tasks and work, but rather teach them to long for the endless immensity of the sea."
– Antoine de Saint-Exupéry, French writer

An often-overlooked blessing: A crisp, new notebook of paper and new pens at the start of a new school year.

Today I am looking forward to . . .

1. _____
2. _____
3. _____
4. _____
5. _____

Today I am grateful for . . .

1. _____
2. _____
3. _____
4. _____
5. _____

Day 110

Today's date: _____

"If you ever find yourself in the wrong story, leave."
— **Mo Willems,** author

Thank you for hard labor and work projects for family members.

Today I am looking forward to . . .

1. _____
2. _____
3. _____
4. _____
5. _____

Today I am grateful for . . .

1. _____
2. _____
3. _____
4. _____
5. _____

Self-Reflection Journal

Day 111

Today's date: _____

"I have no special talents. I am only passionately curious."
— **Albert Einstein**, physicist

An often-overlooked blessing: A jet ski zipping across the water.

Today I am looking forward to . . .

1. _____
2. _____
3. _____
4. _____
5. _____

Today I am grateful for . . .

1. _____
2. _____
3. _____
4. _____
5. _____

Day 112

Today's date: _____

*"It is never too late to be
what you might have been."*
– George Eliot, English novelist

Thank you for a clear night with stars in the morning sky.

Today I am looking forward to . . .

1. _____
2. _____
3. _____
4. _____
5. _____

Today I am grateful for . . .

1. _____
2. _____
3. _____
4. _____
5. _____

Self-Reflection Journal

Day 113

Today's date: _____

"Real courage is when you know you're licked before you begin, but you begin anyway and see it through no matter what."
– Harper Lee, American novelist

An often-overlooked blessing: Open windows at night and the birds waking me up at 4:45 A.M.

Today I am looking forward to . . .

1. _____
2. _____
3. _____
4. _____
5. _____

Today I am grateful for . . .

1. _____
2. _____
3. _____
4. _____
5. _____

Day 114

Today's date: _____

"Only in the darkness can you see the stars."
– Dr. Martin Luther King, Jr.,
activist, preacher, Nobel Peace Prize winner

Thank you for a new day dawning.

Today I am looking forward to . . .

1. _____
2. _____
3. _____
4. _____
5. _____

Today I am grateful for . . .

1. _____
2. _____
3. _____
4. _____
5. _____

Self-Reflection Journal

Day 115

Today's date: _____

"Imagination is the air of the mind."
– Philip James Bailey, English poet

An often-overlooked blessing: Giving to a local charity.

Today I am looking forward to . . .

1. _____
2. _____
3. _____
4. _____
5. _____

Today I am grateful for . . .

1. _____
2. _____
3. _____
4. _____
5. _____

Day 116

Today's date: _____

"No need to hurry, no need to sparkle, no need to be anyone but oneself."
– Virginia Woolf, English writer

Thank you for sending off clothes to be worn by someone who really needs a lift.

Today I am looking forward to . . .

1. _____
2. _____
3. _____
4. _____
5. _____

Today I am grateful for . . .

1. _____
2. _____
3. _____
4. _____
5. _____

Self-Reflection Journal

Day 117

Today's date: _____

"Dismiss whatever insults your own soul."
– **Walt Whitman,** American poet

An often-overlooked blessing: Sports figures who inspire; specifically, Michael Jordan's legacy in basketball.

Today I am looking forward to . . .

1. _____
2. _____
3. _____
4. _____
5. _____

Today I am grateful for . . .

1. _____
2. _____
3. _____
4. _____
5. _____

The Educator's 180-Day Gratitude Turnaround

Day 118

Today's date: _____

"The question isn't who is going to let me; it's who is going to stop me."
– Ayn Rand, Russian philosopher

Thank you for the last dance of a wedding party.

Today I am looking forward to . . .

1. _____
2. _____
3. _____
4. _____
5. _____

Today I am grateful for . . .

1. _____
2. _____
3. _____
4. _____
5. _____

Self-Reflection Journal

Day 119

Today's date: _____

"The sun shines not on us but in us."
— John Muir, naturalist

An often-overlooked blessing: The silver lining of quality family time during the Covid-19 pandemic, and how we navigated through it via distance learning at a rare time in history.

Today I am looking forward to . . .

1. _____
2. _____
3. _____
4. _____
5. _____

Today I am grateful for . . .

1. _____
2. _____
3. _____
4. _____
5. _____

The Educator's 180-Day Gratitude Turnaround

Day 120

Today's date: _____

"An awake heart is like a sky that pours light."
— **Hafiz**, Persian poet

*Thank you for shutting down to power
back up . . . in computers and in life.*

Today I am looking forward to . . .

1. _____
2. _____
3. _____
4. _____
5. _____

Today I am grateful for . . .

1. _____
2. _____
3. _____
4. _____
5. _____

Self-Reflection Journal

Day 121

Today's date: _____

"It is only with the heart that one can see rightly; what is essential is invisible to the eye."
– Antoine de Saint-Exupéry, French author

An often-overlooked blessing: What disease shows us about living differently.

Today I am looking forward to . . .

1. _____
2. _____
3. _____
4. _____
5. _____

Today I am grateful for . . .

1. _____
2. _____
3. _____
4. _____
5. _____

The Educator's 180-Day Gratitude Turnaround

Day 122

Today's date: _____

"No one ever became poor by giving."
– Anne Frank, German-born diarist

Thank you for how science informs our habits.

Today I am looking forward to . . .

1. _____
2. _____
3. _____
4. _____
5. _____

Today I am grateful for . . .

1. _____
2. _____
3. _____
4. _____
5. _____

Self-Reflection Journal

Day 123

Today's date: _____

"I am a great believer in luck, and I find the harder I work, the more I have of it."
– Thomas Jefferson, third U.S. president

An often-overlooked blessing: Fervent prayer that takes your breath away.

Today I am looking forward to . . .

1. _____
2. _____
3. _____
4. _____
5. _____

Today I am grateful for . . .

1. _____
2. _____
3. _____
4. _____
5. _____

The Educator's 180-Day Gratitude Turnaround

Day 124

Today's date: _____

"The most radiant woman in the room is the one full of life and experience."
– Sharon Stone, actress

Thank you for a marriage that gets better every year.

Today I am looking forward to . . .

1. _____
2. _____
3. _____
4. _____
5. _____

Today I am grateful for . . .

1. _____
2. _____
3. _____
4. _____
5. _____

Self-Reflection Journal

Day 125

Today's date: _____

"The one fact that I would cry from every housetop is this: the Good Life is waiting for us—here and now."
– B. F. Skinner, psychologist

An often-overlooked blessing: Working on a book to be published with a cover artist you admire.

Today I am looking forward to . . .

1. _____
2. _____
3. _____
4. _____
5. _____

Today I am grateful for . . .

1. _____
2. _____
3. _____
4. _____
5. _____

Day 126

Today's date: _____

"Out of clutter, find simplicity."
— Albert Einstein, physicist

Thank you for cold weather, dying leaves, and change.

Today I am looking forward to . . .

1. _____
2. _____
3. _____
4. _____
5. _____

Today I am grateful for . . .

1. _____
2. _____
3. _____
4. _____
5. _____

Self-Reflection Journal

Day 127

Today's date: _____

"In order that people may be happy in their work, these three things are needed: They must be fit for it. They must not do too much of it. And they must have a sense of success in it."
– **John Ruskin,** painter, critic

An often-overlooked blessing: Spring time, water rushing as snow melts, and we see the trace of a lawn.

Today I am looking forward to . . .

1. _____
2. _____
3. _____
4. _____
5. _____

Today I am grateful for . . .

1. _____
2. _____
3. _____
4. _____
5. _____

Day 128

Today's date: _____

"Today a new sun rises for me; everything lives, everything is animated, everything seems to speak to me of my passion, everything invites me to cherish it."
— **Anne de Lenclos,** French author

Thank you for the moon this evening and the clear skies and stars.

Today I am looking forward to . . .

1. _____
2. _____
3. _____
4. _____
5. _____

Today I am grateful for . . .

1. _____
2. _____
3. _____
4. _____
5. _____

Self-Reflection Journal

Day 129

Today's date: _____

"Taking joy in life is a woman's best cosmetic."
— **Rosalind Russell,** actress

*An often-overlooked blessing: The rush
of wind and fresh air to breathe in.*

Today I am looking forward to . . .

1. _____
2. _____
3. _____
4. _____
5. _____

Today I am grateful for . . .

1. _____
2. _____
3. _____
4. _____
5. _____

The Educator's 180-Day Gratitude Turnaround

Day 130

Today's date: _____

"Intuition is a spiritual faculty, and does not explain but simply points the way."
– Florence Scovel Shinn, American artist

Thank you for no opinions on outside issues and that my classroom can be a safe place for all points of view and safe sharing and listening.

Today I am looking forward to . . .

1. _____
2. _____
3. _____
4. _____
5. _____

Today I am grateful for . . .

1. _____
2. _____
3. _____
4. _____
5. _____

Self-Reflection Journal

Day 131

Today's date: _____

"Perhaps too much of everything is as bad as too little."
— **Edna Ferber,** American novelist

An often-overlooked blessing: People who by their own example teach us boundaries on speaking, listening, and communicating.

Today I am looking forward to . . .

1. _____
2. _____
3. _____
4. _____
5. _____

Today I am grateful for . . .

1. _____
2. _____
3. _____
4. _____
5. _____

The Educator's 180-Day Gratitude Turnaround

Day 132

Today's date: _____

"Listening to your heart is not simple. Finding out who you are is not simple. It takes a lot of hard work and courage to get to know who you are and what you want."
– Sue Bender, author, ceramic artist

Thank you for the people in my life who make me think new beliefs that empower me and those around me.

Today I am looking forward to . . .

1. _____
2. _____
3. _____
4. _____
5. _____

Today I am grateful for . . .

1. _____
2. _____
3. _____
4. _____
5. _____

Self-Reflection Journal

Day 133

Today's date: _____

*"Some cause happiness wherever they go,
others whenever they go."*
– Oscar Wilde, poet, playwright

An often-overlooked blessing: Perspective and the chance to do something different today outside my comfort zone.

Today I am looking forward to . . .

1. _____
2. _____
3. _____
4. _____
5. _____

Today I am grateful for . . .

1. _____
2. _____
3. _____
4. _____
5. _____

Day 134

Today's date: _____

"If a child doesn't learn the way you teach, teach the way the child learns."
– Eunice Kennedy Shriver, founder, Special Olympics

Thank you for the beautiful sunrise, giant clouds wrapping the sky, and connections to colors.

Today I am looking forward to . . .

1. _____
2. _____
3. _____
4. _____
5. _____

Today I am grateful for . . .

1. _____
2. _____
3. _____
4. _____
5. _____

Self-Reflection Journal

Day 135

Today's date: _____

*"Whatever your past has been,
you have a spotless future."*
– Jo Connor, actress

*An often-overlooked blessing: Saved voicemail
messages that give us hope, joy, and laughter.*

Today I am looking forward to . . .

1. _____
2. _____
3. _____
4. _____
5. _____

Today I am grateful for . . .

1. _____
2. _____
3. _____
4. _____
5. _____

The Educator's 180-Day Gratitude Turnaround

Day 136

Today's date: _____

"Expensive silk ties are the only ones that attract spaghetti sauce."
– Anonymous

Thank you for the many seasons of change and the traditions of connection that bind us together.

Today I am looking forward to . . .

1. _____
2. _____
3. _____
4. _____
5. _____

Today I am grateful for . . .

1. _____
2. _____
3. _____
4. _____
5. _____

Self-Reflection Journal

Day 137

Today's date: _____

"We are what we repeatedly do. Excellence therefore, is not an act, but a habit."
— **Aristotle,** philosopher

An often-overlooked blessing: Partnership, caring, and listening to one another's hopes and dreams.

Today I am looking forward to . . .

1. _____
2. _____
3. _____
4. _____
5. _____

Today I am grateful for . . .

1. _____
2. _____
3. _____
4. _____
5. _____

The Educator's 180-Day Gratitude Turnaround

Day 138

Today's date: _____

"The emotion and narratives you attach to anything can literally change what you see, taste, touch, and feel."
– Ruben Perez, educator

Thank you for the time to daydream today and consider possibilities.

Today I am looking forward to . . .

1. _____
2. _____
3. _____
4. _____
5. _____

Today I am grateful for . . .

1. _____
2. _____
3. _____
4. _____
5. _____

Self-Reflection Journal

Day 139

Today's date: _____

"Children know how to learn in more ways than we know how to teach them."
— **Maria Montessori,** Italian physician, educator

An often-overlooked blessing: Long-time friendships and people who are genuinely there for me through it all.

Today I am looking forward to . . .

1. _____
2. _____
3. _____
4. _____
5. _____

Today I am grateful for . . .

1. _____
2. _____
3. _____
4. _____
5. _____

Day 140

Today's date: _____

"Never tell people how to do things. Tell them what to do, and they will surprise you with their ingenuity."
– Gen. George S. Patton, World War II hero

Thank you for faith, action, works, and deeds that feel good and serve others.

Today I am looking forward to . . .

1. _____
2. _____
3. _____
4. _____
5. _____

Today I am grateful for . . .

1. _____
2. _____
3. _____
4. _____
5. _____

Self-Reflection Journal

Day 141

Today's date: _____

"Nothing is so astonishing as the amount of ignorance it accumulates in the form of inert facts."
– Henry Adams, American historian

An often-overlooked blessing: Teachers and students who listen and respond with love.

Today I am looking forward to . . .

1. _____
2. _____
3. _____
4. _____
5. _____

Today I am grateful for . . .

1. _____
2. _____
3. _____
4. _____
5. _____

Day 142

Today's date: _____

"The trouble with facts is that there are so many of them."
— Samuel Crothers, minister, essayist

Thank you for best-selling books and music and words/practices that unify.

Today I am looking forward to . . .

1. _____
2. _____
3. _____
4. _____
5. _____

Today I am grateful for . . .

1. _____
2. _____
3. _____
4. _____
5. _____

Self-Reflection Journal

Day 143

Today's date: _____

"Man's business here is to know for the sake of living, not to live for the sake of knowing."
– Frederic Harrison, British historian

An often-overlooked blessing: Courage to listen, even when it's hard work.

Today I am looking forward to . . .

1. _____
2. _____
3. _____
4. _____
5. _____

Today I am grateful for . . .

1. _____
2. _____
3. _____
4. _____
5. _____

Day 144

Today's date: _____

"Work consists of whatever a body is obliged to do. Play consists of whatever a body is not obliged to do."
– Mark Twain

Thank you for helping me keep my mouth shut; to respond in a kinder, gentler way.

Today I am looking forward to . . .

1. _____
2. _____
3. _____
4. _____
5. _____

Today I am grateful for . . .

1. _____
2. _____
3. _____
4. _____
5. _____

Self-Reflection Journal

Day 145

Today's date: _____

"Nobody is bored when he is trying to make something that is beautiful, or to discover something that is true."
– William Inge, American playwright

An often-overlooked blessing: The amazing gift of air travel, that in three hours I can travel what would take twelve hours in a car.

Today I am looking forward to . . .

1. _____
2. _____
3. _____
4. _____
5. _____

Today I am grateful for . . .

1. _____
2. _____
3. _____
4. _____
5. _____

Day 146

Today's date: _____

"I complained that I had no shoes, until I met a man who had no feet."
– Anonymous

Thank you for cooler, crisp weather, changing leaves, and the contrast of seasons.

Today I am looking forward to . . .

1. _____
2. _____
3. _____
4. _____
5. _____

Today I am grateful for . . .

1. _____
2. _____
3. _____
4. _____
5. _____

Self-Reflection Journal

Day 147

Today's date: _____

"The intelligence is proved not by ease of learning but by understanding what we learn."
– Joseph Whitney, professor of geography

An often-overlooked blessing: A cabin in northern Minnesota; the blue water's reflection.

Today I am looking forward to . . .

1. _____
2. _____
3. _____
4. _____
5. _____

Today I am grateful for . . .

1. _____
2. _____
3. _____
4. _____
5. _____

Day 148

Today's date: _____

"If you want to see what children can do, you must stop giving them things."
– Norman Douglas, British writer

Thank you for knowing deep down that all is well in my soul.

Today I am looking forward to . . .

1. _____
2. _____
3. _____
4. _____
5. _____

Today I am grateful for . . .

1. _____
2. _____
3. _____
4. _____
5. _____

Self-Reflection Journal

Day 149

Today's date: _____

"As soon as you trust yourself, you will know how to live."
– **Goethe,** German writer

An often-overlooked blessing: The bubbles in the soap as you wash dishes.

Today I am looking forward to . . .

1. _____
2. _____
3. _____
4. _____
5. _____

Today I am grateful for . . .

1. _____
2. _____
3. _____
4. _____
5. _____

The Educator's 180-Day Gratitude Turnaround

Day 150

Today's date: _____

"The secret of being a bore is to tell everything."
– Voltaire, French writer

*Thank you for singing on the way
to work, the energy of each chorus.*

Today I am looking forward to . . .

1. _____
2. _____
3. _____
4. _____
5. _____

Today I am grateful for . . .

1. _____
2. _____
3. _____
4. _____
5. _____

Self-Reflection Journal

Day 151

Today's date: _____

"No instrument smaller than the world is fit to measure men and women. Examinations measure the examinee."
— **Sir Walter Raleigh,** English writer

An often-overlooked blessing: That on the way to work I see sunshine today.

Today I am looking forward to . . .

1. _____
2. _____
3. _____
4. _____
5. _____

Today I am grateful for . . .

1. _____
2. _____
3. _____
4. _____
5. _____

The Educator's 180-Day Gratitude Turnaround

Day 152

Today's date: _____

"He was so learned, that he could name a horse in nine languages. So ignorant that he bought a cow to ride on."
– **Benjamin Franklin,** American statesman

Thank you for nature, trees, branches; vibrant green, brown, and yellows.

Today I am looking forward to . . .

1. _____
2. _____
3. _____
4. _____
5. _____

Today I am grateful for . . .

1. _____
2. _____
3. _____
4. _____
5. _____

Self-Reflection Journal

Day 153

Today's date: _____

"Success is not a magic ingredient that can be supplied by teachers. Building on strengths allows students to create their own success."
– Robert Martin, software engineer

An often-overlooked blessing: For the spaces, in our homes, small or large, that we live in—that less is more.

Today I am looking forward to . . .

1. _____
2. _____
3. _____
4. _____
5. _____

Today I am grateful for . . .

1. _____
2. _____
3. _____
4. _____
5. _____

The Educator's 180-Day Gratitude Turnaround

Day 154

Today's date: _____

"So that in order that a man may be happy, it is necessary that he should not only be capable of his work, but be a good judge of his work."
– **John Ruskin,** English painter, crtic

Thank you for the abundance we have in a free education.

Today I am looking forward to . . .

1. _____
2. _____
3. _____
4. _____
5. _____

Today I am grateful for . . .

1. _____
2. _____
3. _____
4. _____
5. _____

Self-Reflection Journal

Day 155

Today's date: _____

"I always tell my students at the beginning of the semester: if they don't learn, it's my fault."
– **John Bowyer**, colonel in English Civil War

An often-overlooked blessing: Thank you for Google.

Today I am looking forward to . . .

1. _____
2. _____
3. _____
4. _____
5. _____

Today I am grateful for . . .

1. _____
2. _____
3. _____
4. _____
5. _____

The Educator's 180-Day Gratitude Turnaround

Day 156

Today's date: _____

"I am the master of everything I can explain."
– Theodore Haecker, German writer

Thank you for how technology connects us.

Today I am looking forward to . . .

1. _____
2. _____
3. _____
4. _____
5. _____

Today I am grateful for . . .

1. _____
2. _____
3. _____
4. _____
5. _____

Self-Reflection Journal

Day 157

Today's date: _____

"We shall require a substantially new manner of thinking if mankind is to survive."
– Albert Einstein

An often-overlooked blessing: Professional and personal learning community where one can learn, grow, and discover new ideas that impact children for the better.

Today I am looking forward to . . .

1. _____
2. _____
3. _____
4. _____
5. _____

Today I am grateful for . . .

1. _____
2. _____
3. _____
4. _____
5. _____

Day 158

Today's date: _____

*"Wise men learn more from
fools than fools from wise men."*
– Cato, Roman soldier, historian

*Thank you for positive behavior and
the courage to be self-reflective.*

Today I am looking forward to . . .

1. _____
2. _____
3. _____
4. _____
5. _____

Today I am grateful for . . .

1. _____
2. _____
3. _____
4. _____
5. _____

Self-Reflection Journal

Day 159

Today's date: _____

"In teaching the greatest sin is to be boring."
— **J. F. Herbart,** German philosopher

An often-overlooked blessing: Relationships that sharpen our ideals and practices to get better, every day.

Today I am looking forward to . . .

1. _____
2. _____
3. _____
4. _____
5. _____

Today I am grateful for . . .

1. _____
2. _____
3. _____
4. _____
5. _____

The Educator's 180-Day Gratitude Turnaround

Day 160

Today's date: _____

"People always told me that my natural ability and good eyesight were the reasons for my success as a hitter. They never talk about practice, practice, practice!"
– **Ted Williams,** baseball player

Thank you for the support of community members, neighbors.

Today I am looking forward to . . .

1. _____
2. _____
3. _____
4. _____
5. _____

Today I am grateful for . . .

1. _____
2. _____
3. _____
4. _____
5. _____

Self-Reflection Journal

Day 161

Today's date: _____

"Anytime you see a turtle up on top of a fence post, you know he had some help."
– Alex Haley, author

An often-overlooked blessing: The small act of kindness in opening the door.

Today I am looking forward to . . .

1. _____
2. _____
3. _____
4. _____
5. _____

Today I am grateful for . . .

1. _____
2. _____
3. _____
4. _____
5. _____

The Educator's 180-Day Gratitude Turnaround

Day 162

Today's date: _____

"An unusual amount of common
sense is sometimes called 'wisdom'."
– Clare Jackson, senior tutor, Cambridge University

*Thank you for holding the door
open so we can all come in together.*

Today I am looking forward to . . .

1. _____
2. _____
3. _____
4. _____
5. _____

Today I am grateful for . . .

1. _____
2. _____
3. _____
4. _____
5. _____

Self-Reflection Journal

Day 163

Today's date: _____

"Prove that you can control yourself, and you are an educated person, and without this all other education is good for nothing."
– R. D. Hitchcock, author

An often-overlooked blessing: Support groups that connect new students who have just moved into the district.

Today I am looking forward to . . .

1. _____
2. _____
3. _____
4. _____
5. _____

Today I am grateful for . . .

1. _____
2. _____
3. _____
4. _____
5. _____

Day 164

Today's date: _____

"Do what you can, with what you have, where you are. What better can you do?"
– Theodore Roosevelt, twenty-sixth U.S. president

Thank you for teachers who practice gratitude within themselves, as that spills over into their day in a healthy way.

Today I am looking forward to . . .

1. _____
2. _____
3. _____
4. _____
5. _____

Today I am grateful for . . .

1. _____
2. _____
3. _____
4. _____
5. _____

Self-Reflection Journal

Day 165

Today's date: _____

"Everything's holy, everything, even me."
– John Steinbeck, author

An often-overlooked blessing: Parents who get kids ready for school each day.

Today I am looking forward to . . .

1. _____
2. _____
3. _____
4. _____
5. _____

Today I am grateful for . . .

1. _____
2. _____
3. _____
4. _____
5. _____

Day 166

Today's date: _____

"The person who finds no satisfaction in themselves seeks for it in vain elsewhere."
– F. La Rochefoucauld, French author

Thank you for balanced, healthy school lunches that focus on nutrition.

Today I am looking forward to . . .

1. _____
2. _____
3. _____
4. _____
5. _____

Today I am grateful for . . .

1. _____
2. _____
3. _____
4. _____
5. _____

Self-Reflection Journal

Day 167

Today's date: _____

"Because the reteaching is brief, few students are likely to be bored. It may be too late already, but it's not as much too late now as it will be later."
– **C. H. Weisert**, educator

An often-overlooked blessing: Knowing and believing that synergy always wins.

Today I am looking forward to . . .

1. _____
2. _____
3. _____
4. _____
5. _____

Today I am grateful for . . .

1. _____
2. _____
3. _____
4. _____
5. _____

Day 168

Today's date: _____

"The worst sin toward our fellow creatures is not to hate them, but to be indifferent to them; that's the essence of inhumanity."
– George Bernard Shaw, Irish playwright

Thank you for the humility that leaders have in not taking all the credit when something goes well. They acknowledge the team and raise up the team.

Today I am looking forward to . . .

1. _____
2. _____
3. _____
4. _____
5. _____

Today I am grateful for . . .

1. _____
2. _____
3. _____
4. _____
5. _____

Self-Reflection Journal

Day 169

Today's date: _____

"Children are living messages we send into the future, a future that we will not see. In effect we are building the house of tomorrow day by day, not out of bricks or steel, but out of the stuff of children's bodies, hearts and minds."
– Melvin Konner, educator

An often-overlooked blessing: Collective teacher efficacy and the power of teams who, together, offer their ideas to make great kids greater.

Today I am looking forward to . . .

1. _____
2. _____
3. _____
4. _____
5. _____

Today I am grateful for . . .

1. _____
2. _____
3. _____
4. _____
5. _____

Day 170

Today's date: _____

*"In our differences, we grow;
in our sameness, we connect."*
– Virginia Satir, American author

Thank you for end-of-year excitement, planning, and chaos.

Today I am looking forward to . . .

1. _____
2. _____
3. _____
4. _____
5. _____

Today I am grateful for . . .

1. _____
2. _____
3. _____
4. _____
5. _____

Self-Reflection Journal

Day 171

Today's date: _____

"When in doubt, tell the truth."
— Mark Twain, writer

An often-overlooked blessing: The "I am listening for your greatness" type of friendships. Being heard is one of the greatest gifts.

Today I am looking forward to . . .

1. _____
2. _____
3. _____
4. _____
5. _____

Today I am grateful for . . .

1. _____
2. _____
3. _____
4. _____
5. _____

Day 172

Today's date: _____

"The cynics may be the loudest voices, but I promise you, they will accomplish the least."
– Barack Obama, forty-fourth U.S. president

Thank you for farms, green grass, and the white fences that line certain homes with a particular intention of harmony created in those spaces.

Today I am looking forward to . . .

1. _____
2. _____
3. _____
4. _____
5. _____

Today I am grateful for . . .

1. _____
2. _____
3. _____
4. _____
5. _____

Self-Reflection Journal

Day 173

Today's date: _____

"Intelligence appears to be the thing that enables a man to get along without education. Education enables a man to get along without the use of his intelligence."
– Albert Edwards Wiggam, analyst

An often-overlooked blessing: Books, literature, and writing; speaking and presenting; and the ability to communicate ideas and messages with flair and goodwill.

Today I am looking forward to . . .

1. _____
2. _____
3. _____
4. _____
5. _____

Today I am grateful for . . .

1. _____
2. _____
3. _____
4. _____
5. _____

The Educator's 180-Day Gratitude Turnaround

Day 174

Today's date: _____

"The school where my father was principal, you couldn't drop out. You could leave, but he went and got you."
— **Asa Hilliard**, professor of educational psychology

Thank you for the students who became readers this year, and the first-grade teachers who are heroes of learning to read.

Today I am looking forward to . . .

1. _____
2. _____
3. _____
4. _____
5. _____

Today I am grateful for . . .

1. _____
2. _____
3. _____
4. _____
5. _____

Self-Reflection Journal

Day 175

Today's date: _____

"Be confident, for the stars are of the same stuff as you."
– Nikolaj Velimirovic, poet

An often-overlooked blessing: The ways we closed the learning gap this year with so many students and teachers who show their care in action.

Today I am looking forward to . . .

1. _____
2. _____
3. _____
4. _____
5. _____

Today I am grateful for . . .

1. _____
2. _____
3. _____
4. _____
5. _____

Day 176

Today's date: _____

"The first requirement for growth of the individual is that the person remain in touch with his own perceptions."
– Clark Moustakas, American psychologist

Thank you for the newness of each day and the hope that is brought forth in mindsets that empower us to see each other without judgment.

Today I am looking forward to . . .

1. _____
2. _____
3. _____
4. _____
5. _____

Today I am grateful for . . .

1. _____
2. _____
3. _____
4. _____
5. _____

Self-Reflection Journal

Day 177

Today's date: _____

"The secret of education is respecting the pupil."
– Ralph Waldo Emerson, essayist

An often-overlooked blessing: Relationships that are mended, and forgiveness that reigns over past hurts.

Today I am looking forward to . . .

1. _____
2. _____
3. _____
4. _____
5. _____

Today I am grateful for . . .

1. _____
2. _____
3. _____
4. _____
5. _____

Day 178

Today's date: _____

"What can be done at any time is never done at all."
– English proverb

Thank you for not staying stagnant and still; for being willing to fail forward, learn, and grow.

Today I am looking forward to . . .

1. _____
2. _____
3. _____
4. _____
5. _____

Today I am grateful for . . .

1. _____
2. _____
3. _____
4. _____
5. _____

Self-Reflection Journal

Day 179

Today's date: _____

"If you hear that someone is speaking ill of you, instead of trying to defend yourself, say, 'They obviously do not know me, since there are so many other faults he could have mentioned'."
– Epictetus, Greek philosopher

An often-overlooked blessing: The ability to adjust to all the new norms this year, and build new skill sets.

Today I am looking forward to . . .

1. _____
2. _____
3. _____
4. _____
5. _____

Today I am grateful for . . .

1. _____
2. _____
3. _____
4. _____
5. _____

The Educator's 180-Day Gratitude Turnaround

Day 180

Today's date: _____

"I was successful because you believed in me."
— **Gen. Ulysses S. Grant,**
speaking to President Abraham Lincoln

Thank you for knowing I did my best today, and every time I want to get better at something I stop, self-reflect, and take a new action going forward, once again.

Today I am looking forward to . . .

1. _____
2. _____
3. _____
4. _____
5. _____

Today I am grateful for . . .

1. _____
2. _____
3. _____
4. _____
5. _____

Closing Thoughts

You made it! Congrats!
Each entry is a gift; each set of gratitudes a start toward peace and hope.

How do you feel about the process?
What do you think about your experience?
Were the time, effort, and energy worth it?
What did you learn?
I'd love to connect with you on the experience.
Please contact me in some form:

Web site: JennySeverson.com
Email: jeniferjseverson@gmail.com
Facebook: Jenny Severson
Instagram: @dr.jenny.severson
Twitter: @severson_j

Go ahead and hit me up with a text, post, tag, or email. I'd love to hear how this experience was for you. Using social media will also connect you to a larger network on this topic, so go ahead and reach out.

I hope you enjoyed this self-reflection journal and, if you did, I would very much appreciate it if you would share your thoughts on social media and tag me, then head over to Amazon.com, and write a review of this book.

Not only does it make my day to see you and what you are up to, it allows us to connect and build a community of hope, optimism, and grateful hearts.

Pass It On

The *Educator's 180-Day Gratitude Turnaround: Self-Reflection Journal* was written for you, the human being behind the title of teacher, educator, superintendent, parent, principal, assistant principal, instructional coach, director of instruction, custodial staff, support staff, and anyone else in the field of education. Including parents!

If you like what you see here, please pass it on, please share, follow, and connect me to your tribe of colleagues, friends, and associates. How much fun would it be to create a community of more grateful educators?

Never miss a chance to see what is good, pure, right, and connected in your classroom, community, and life, for this is where the juice and joy of life reside.

Gratitude is a great way to start to hardwire new thoughts in your life and act upon them each day.

I was looking for a way to help you recognize the gratitude and optimism that surround you at any given time. As I shared in my own story and journey of life, I went from surviving to thriving only because of where I placed my focus and attention. This is a daily practice to engage our hearts and minds.

I often say, "Where the attention goes, the energy flows." The positive impact you are making on those around you starts with writing it down and then, hopefully, amplifying it in voice each day. Keeping track, reflecting, and making this a habit is a game changer for you and your life.

Gratitude, which in turn leads to the legacy you are creating, is never something you regret making time for. . . . you only want more. That's why we created this resource, so you can, day after day, week after week, month after month, year after year, take those few minutes each day to see yourself and your impact, and to express gratitude.

Whether it is students in your classroom, teachers on your campus, or entire districts you are influencing, you are leaving a legacy. Be aware of that legacy and impact. Be deliberate about creating the footprint that helps you see the gratitude and optimism around you each day.

A note to everyone on the journey: We all veer off course, and sometimes you might not be able to see what you are creating. That is the nature of human development, especially with kids growing up in front of us. This self-reflection gratitude journal is a book for you to record the positive impact you are making with those around you. If you are a teacher, you can write about student growth. If you are a leader in your district, you can write about how you are helping others achieve their dreams and desires. If you are support staff, you can write about how your job is leaving a positive impact on the people you support.

Focusing on the positives will help you get through the year and help you realize the value you provide to others.

Purposefully looking at the value you bring and the opportunities for growth will give you the confidence you need to continue your educator's journey.

When you are having a challenging day, read some of the entries you made. It shows your growth when you record the items over time. Work at it! It works when you show up to practice each day.

Remember . . . progress, not perfection!

My goal in this offering is for you to know that you matter! You are loved, valued, and respected.

I am walking and teaching with you today.

May God bless you, always!
Jenny

Printed in the USA
CPSIA information can be obtained
at www.ICGtesting.com
LVHW041151210324
775094LV00001B/108